To   Gill

From Molly with many
fond memories of a decade
spent together, which you
helped make a happy,
pleasurable and interesting
experience for me in Toronto.

With love and Best Wishes
to one English / British / Canadian
Catophile from another Manx /
British / Canadian Catophile

The Definitive Cheshire Cat

The Definitive Cheshire Cat

O. F. W. Fisher

Pentland Books
Durham – Edinburgh – Oxford

© O.F.W. Fisher, 2000

First published in 2000 by
The Pentland Books Ltd
1 Hutton Close
South Church
Bishop Auckland
Durham

Email: manuscripts@pentlandpress.co.uk
Web: www.pentlandpress.co.uk

ISBN 1–85821-854–3

Typeset in Adobe Garamond 11 on 13
by Carnegie Publishing
Carnegie House
Chatsworth Road
Lancaster

Web: www.carnegiepub.co.uk

Printed and bound by
Antony Rowe Ltd
Chippenham

Dedicated to my Familiars:

Leicester, Rustem, Acat, Pangur Ban, Ffinlo, Geff, Phes, and Saturn.

Contents

Illustrations

Illustrations

Introduction

FROM EARLIEST TIMES the cat was worshipped and held in the highest esteem as a focus of mystic power and reverence; like all deities, it was represented in pictorial and sculptural forms. The first pictorial representations so far located are believed to be on an Egyptian tomb circa 2000 BC with domestic records from 1800 BC.

Perhaps the first statuettes of cats were those found in Hacilar in Turkish Anatolia. These are reputed to date from 600 BC, some 570 years before the superb 'Gayer-Anderson Cat' (30 BC) now in the British Museum. This latter is wearing a nose ring and crescent shaped gold ear-rings, after the style of the god Bast.

The archetypal Cheshire Cat as depicted today, in both pictorial and sculptural form, has the following salient features: a wide grinning mouth, stretching from ear to ear and containing a multiplicity of sharp teeth, the head is wide like a Persian cat, the neck is of exaggerated length. It is a magical cat and is reputed to be able to disappear, either in part or totally at will. All types of colouration are permitted, when visible to the human eye. Both long and short haired varieties are depicted and have all types of markings.

When I acquired my first two Cheshire Cats in the summer of 1980 at an antique fair in Moggerhanger from an appropriate Cheshire dealer I first ascertained their date of 1899, and then wished to know the origin of the Cheshire Cat. To quote the Oxford Dictionary: "Undetermined Origin" (1770–1855). Twelve years later, I have been able to ascertain most of the facts behind the inception and subsequent development of the Cheshire Cat up to the present day.

O.F.W. Fisher.

Acknowledgements

THE AUTHOR WISHES TO THANK the following, who have been helpful in the preparation of this work: F. Hughes, The British Museum, Bizarre Acres Publication, University of Oslo, BBC Television, Kodak Ltd., Garrard & Co. Ltd., Council of the City of Chester, Bedfordshire County Library, The Bishop of Chester, Grays Pottery, A. Oakes, City of Chester Records, G. Webster, R. Holland, Cheshire Records Office, J.C. Bridge, W.E.A. Axon, J.E. Gordon Cartlidge, Cheshire Historian, T.W. Barlow, Cheshire & Lancs. Historical Collector, The Guardian, Grosvenor Museum, Douglas Public Library, Phillips, The Manx Museum and National Trust, Royal Doulton, Murray Sons and Co. Ltd. Figs. 2 and 32 are reproduced by permission of the Royal Mail. The cover illustration is reproduced by kind permission of Kodak Ltd.

Chapter One

"To Grin Like a Cheshire Cat"

OVER THE YEARS MUCH SPECULATION has taken place regarding the origin of this famous expression which is still in common use today, just as it was in the distant past. The first located written reference is dated 1770–1819 Wolcott (P. Pinder) "Lo! Like a Cheshire Cat our court will grin."

In 1808 a letter dated the 26 February, was sent from C. Lamb to Manning. In it was the following: "I made a pun the other day, and palmed it upon Holcroft, who grinned like a Cheshire Cat."

In 1855 Thackeray wrote: "Menna is smiling with all her might. In fact Mr Newcombe says that woman grins like a Cheshire Cat."

In 1865 Dodgson first published his famous children's book, *Alice in Wonderland*, dated 1866 after the fashion of the time. It will be noted that the expression was in common usage more than a hundred years before his time. How far back in time we will see, in a later chapter.

Charles Lutwidge Dodgson was born at Daresbury parsonage on 27 January 1832 and died at Guildford on 14 January 1898. A stained glass window commemorating his life is in Daresbury Church, Cheshire. (Fig. 1) It will be noted that the head of the famous Cheshire Cat is featured in the centre of the window. Dodgson, writing under the name of Lewis Carroll, published his book privately in 1865 (Dated 1866). He met the famous illustrator John Tenniel in 1863 and Tenniel drew the first definitive popular published Cheshire Cat. Dodgson had done the original cat drawings, but was not happy with the result. By 1870, sales of *Alice in Wonderland* had reached 25,000 copies, all with the famous Tenniel Cheshire Cat illustrations. (See Fig. 2.)

In 1898, the year of Lewis Carroll's death, sales of the book had reached 86,000 in England alone, the book was being translated into many languages and sold all over the world. It has been said that it has been translated into more languages than any other book, with the exception of the Bible.

In 1907, the copyright on *Alice in Wonderland* expired but the book, as popular as ever, was then re-published through many sources and the Cheshire Cat was illustrated by many different talented artists. Amongst the most well known are the following: Arthur Rackham 1907 (Fig. 3.), M.L. Attwell 1910, and Salvador Dali in 1969.

One of these was a particularly charming version of the Cheshire Cat, which was used to illustrate a piece of sheet music entitled: Ye Cheshire Cat – "The Wonderland Quadrilles". This music cover was printed in Chromolithograph, after the style of Tenniel, and is almost an exact replica of the original. (Fig. 4.) The piece was composed for the pianoforte by C.H.R. Marriott circa 1872 and is in the British Library. (h.1359/20).

A great number of possible explanations have been given for the origins of the expression "to grin like a Cheshire cat" and a number of these are now quoted for reference and evaluation purposes, these have been elaborated on as necessary.

In 1852 (*Notes & Queries* p. 402) it states that the Cheshire Cat was based on an unhappy attempt by a Cheshire sign writer to represent a Lion Rampant, which was the crest of an influential family, on the sign boards of many local inns. The resemblance of these lions to cats caused them to be generally called by the more ignoble name. This explanation was propounded by many early researchers, who quoted multiple references to inns, all over the country, where the depicted lion had become known as the cat.

The most popular suggested examples of this phenomenon are the following:

The public house at Charlton between Pewsey and Devises in Wiltshire, which is popularly known as "The Cat at Charlton". The inn was originally known as the Lion or Tiger or some such animal, believed to be based on the crest of Sir Edward Poore.

The Downing Arms near Royston, Hertfordshire, has for many years been known as "The Scratching Cat" and I have an addressed postcard printed by the inn, with the Scratching Cat duly printed under the official name for the address.

The above two examples are located at some distance from Cheshire, but there are others in the locality such as the Cheshire Cat at Nantwich, reputed to be 400 years old, and which used to have a sign featuring a Cheshire Cat, which was removed circa 1980, due to wear and tear.

The much younger Downing Arms, mentioned above was in fact founded by the Cambridge college of the same name in 1827. Originally the sign featured the coat of arms of the college, namely a Griffin Rampant. It has been known as The Scratching Cat, almost since its inception. I spoke to a local who had frequented this pub for 60 years and he told me it had been known as the Scratching Cat long before his time. The front of the building is inscribed with The Downing Arms; while at the side and also on the upright post holding the inn sign is written: The Scratching Cat, derived from the long clawed Griffin. (My visit took place in 1980).

Many of the Cheshire inns used the crest of the Saxon and Norman Earls of Chester. Hugh used an Azure with wolf's head erased Argent and Randle a rampant lion. Fig. 5 depicts the wolf's head, which when badly painted, was supposed to resemble a Cheshire Cat.

It has been suggested that the cats in Cheshire are prone to smile because Cheshire is a county palatine, and on further cogitation of their independent status they grin from ear to ear. It should be borne in mind that in 1933 Cheshire & Lancashire were still Counties Palatine. Previously so were Durham, Pembroke, Hexhamshire & Ely. It has never been suggested that the cats in these counties, having the same status, were sufficiently amused as to grin, or even smile!

Shortly before 1850 Cheshire cheeses were sold, moulded into the shape of a cat. These had bristles inserted to represent whiskers. There is also evidence of these cheeses being sold in Bath.

In the middle ages a Cheshire forest warden by the name of Thomas Caterlain, took pleasure in torturing and killing any poachers caught in his territory. It is said that he made frightful grimaces when torturing his victims, hence "To grin like a Cheshire Caterlain" evolved into "To grin like a Cheshire Cat." This was also supposed to explain why male cats are called Toms.

At Stretton near Warrington, the Lion & Cat are depicted on the same inn sign of the Cat & Lion. Around them on the sign is written:

> The lion is strong,
> The cat is vicious,
> My ale is good,
> And so is my liquors.

Variations on the expression "To grin like a Cheshire Cat" are "To grin like a Cheshire Cat chewing gravel" and "To grin like a Cheshire Cat eating Cheese". The latter is easily explained by the fact that Cheshire is a county famous for its cheese and milk products.

The ability of the Cheshire Cat to converse can be compared to the old tale of The King of the Cats. The earliest form of this curious story was entitled *Beware the Cat* and was first printed in 1551, and subsequently reprinted by Mr. J.O. Halliwell in 1864 (British Museum 12316 C 29).

In the story, a man while riding through Kankwood in Shropshire, was spoken to by a cat which asked him to advise his own cat, when he arrived home, that Grimalkin was dead. The man told his wife the curious cat message, when he arrived home. Subsequently his own cat, which had been listening, looked at him sadly and said: "Grimalkin is dead? Then farewell dame!" The cat then left the house, and was never seen again. This story is also told in a Scandinavian form, in which King Pippe is dead. Another variant current in Lancashire and Cheshire quotes the name of the dead cat as Doldrum.

There is better authenticity for John Catherall of Chester whose coat of arms is dated 1304 and included a cat. He dealt ruthlessly with poachers and robbers in his official capacity as Forester of Mara and it is said that his grin indicated extreme anger. He died grinning in defence of Chester and was buried in the city walls. It will be noted that there is a strong resemblance between this tale and that concerning Thomas Caterlain, as quoted above.

It must also be borne in mind that the term "Grinning" in earlier times often referred to a much more hostile facial expression than it does today. The term used to imply that the person involved was showing his teeth in a ferocious manner, more like a snarling sneer than the humorous implication that is understood today. A quotation from Shakespeare, taken from Richard II, makes the point: "Keeps Death his count and there the antic sits; Scoffing his state and grinning at his pomp."

A secondary cheese related story from a Cheshire source, in the form of an ancient inhabitant of Chester, stated that in days gone by a small cheese, known as a "Cat" was marketed. This cheese, due to its small size, was more prone to shrinkage than the normal cheeses. Due to this phenomenon, the "Cat" cheeses became wrinkled, and suggested the appearance of a Grinning Cat! There are also records of: "Grinning like a Cheeser Cat" applied to cats that are particularly fond of cheese.

Chapter Two

The Cheshire Cat Safari

IN THE SUMMER OF 1980 the author went on a Cheshire Cat Safari to Cheshire and stayed for a time in a small rented cottage in the hamlet of Hampton Heath, near Malpas, overlooked by the Sandstone Way. From this base sorties were made into the surrounding Cheshire countryside in search of the elusive Cheshire Cat.

On the first outing a trip was made to Brimstage in Wirral to see the famous Red Cat. There used to be an inn of that name but the site is now occupied by the Village Hall, which was erected by the First Viscount Leverhulme, the Lord of the Manor. The Village Hall sign incorporates the head of the "Red Cat". (Fig. 6)

In the afternoon we visited Brimstage Hall, which dates back to 1398. In a corner of the stone vaulted chantry chapel is the "Cat". It is located on a corbel and carved in stone. Sadly its resemblance to a cat was only marginal, being more like a mini-demon. (Fig. 7) It certainly looks rather unhappy and it has been suggested that this cat is the source of the idea that Cheshire Cats chew gravel!

Over the church porch at Malpas (Pronounced 'Moll Puss' by the locals) is a gargoyle, which greatly resembles a grinning cat. (Fig. 8) According to the official guide book on the church this is dated about the 15th Century. The grin on this cat is very pronounced and the cat has an exceptionally fine set of long sharp teeth! I was so impressed with this fine Cheshire Cat that it inspired the grin as demonstrated in front of the church! (Fig. 9).

A visit was made on the 20th of August 1980 to the famous Gray's Cheshire Cat pottery, located in the ship inn, Handbridge, Chester, which at that time made the very fine striped tabby type Cheshire Cats.

Christina Gray does the decoration but other work is carried out by the other members of the family. Production is greatly exceeded by demand. One large, one medium and two small Cheshire Cats were duly purchased. The medium cats were made in three forms, two were made observing each other, and the third full face. Fig. 10 shows the Ship Inn, with charmingly decorated delivery Land Rover parked in front. Fig. 11 shows the large version of the Gray's Cheshire Cat, sitting in the snow and happily anticipating the time when the frozen cream on top of the milk thaws!

Fig. 12 shows a gathering of Cheshire cats seated on a century old fairground wagon. The small winking Gray's cat mentioned above is on the far left of the photo, left to right, Ginger Cheshire Cat, with name on collar, (a duplicate on the far right), next the Medium Gray's cat, 1899 Black cat mentioned in the Introduction (See p. 1), large Gray's Cat is sitting in the centre of the group. The Ginger cat was acquired in St Michael's Row, Chester.

By far the most exciting find on the safari was the quite superb and exceedingly old stone carved Cheshire Cat on the church at Grappenhall. (Fig. 13) Facing the front of the church, the cat is located on the left hand outer wall and today grins at the adjoining tavern, from the wall of which the photo was taken. The cat is high on the wall of St Wilfrid's church, above the large west window.

I have been in correspondence with the Bishop of Chester, and he referred me to Raymond Richards' large survey of Cheshire Churches. On p. 168 of that authoritative work one finds the following information:

"…by its grinning expression, it may be the original of the proverbial Cheshire Cat."

It is my personal opinion that this superlative feline is probably the oldest extant specimen of a Cheshire Cat. I feel that it was probably the front of an ancient altar which stood on the site of the present not very ancient church. Just as standing religious stones were commonly incorporated into the fabric of churches, built on similar religious sites in many parts of the country, so this truly remarkable Cheshire Cat was incorporated, high in an inaccessible wall of St Wilfrid's at Grappenhall. In this way, practitioners of the ancient Cheshire Cat worship could not practise their rites as of old. This would also explain why there are virtually no written records as to its origins. It would suit the early Christians on the site to ignore the sacred representations of earlier religions.

It should be mentioned that there is a well known Cheshire Cat head in the 14th-Century church at Pott Shrigley. This is essentially an amiable toothless cat, and in this respect at variance with those described above.

Charles Lutwidge Dodgson was born at Daresbury Parsonage, and it was he who can take most of the credit, through the medium of his *Alice in Wonderland* books for turning an ancient fierce grinning and snarling cat, into an amiable creature of similar countenance. (See Chapter 1) Daresbury is only a very short distance from the village of Grappenhall; it is certain that Dodgson would have been completely familiar with the Grappenhall Cat just described, and due to its proximity, impressive size and great antiquity is much more likely to have used it as a role model for his stories than any other suggested Cheshire Cat. It is certainly thanks to Dodgson that the Cheshire Cat is today known the world over, rather than being known, primarily for its grin, as a quaint English expression. He took "To Grin like a Cheshire Cat", the ancient expression, and made it well known to the world. The Alice books, in turn, encouraged the multiplicity of Cheshire Cat sculptures in all mediums, although the long necks, associated with these sculptures, as we will see in a later chapter, pre-date Dodgson by thousands of years. No long necked cats were used in the Alice books. They show that there was still a remnant of the memory of a much more ancient Cheshire Cat.

It has been suggested that there is a Viking connection, and that some Cheshire Cats invaded England, from the find of a head subsequently found in Greenland. From investigations through the

University of Oslo, and the Viking ship museum in Oslo, various carvings of a cat like nature (s.c. "Spanen") have been investigated; together with carvings from the Oseberg ship. These have proved indeterminate, but generally are more Dragonesque than feline.

A number of Goss figures of relatively modern origin have been examined and one 80mm long is inscribed: "He grins like a Cheshire Cat eating gravel". This perpetuates the old saying, as originally exemplified by the Red Cat of Brimstage, already discussed.

In my Cheshire Cat Collection, is a small Mexican type Cheshire Cat vessel. It is 2¼" high and 2" across the lip. It is made in brown earthenware and the grinning head is opposite the handle. A Grecian type frieze is around the body. On consultation with the British Museum, it was thought to be Oxaca, of undetermined date. (Fig. 14)

Chapter Three

The Cheshire Cat in History

CAT WORSHIP AND TRIBAL TOTEM ANIMALS were common from the earliest times, as discussed in the Introduction, starting with the worship of Bast in Egypt *c.* 2000 B.C. The goddess Bast started as the chief goddess of the eighteenth Nome or province of Lower Egypt in the town of Bubastis. Bubastis can be translated as: "The House of Bast." Bast reached her zenith of importance when in about 950 BC in the 22nd Dynasty, Bubastis became the capital of the kingdom. Her sacred animal was the cat and she is often represented as a cat headed woman, holding a Sistrum in her right hand, a basket in the left. Her importance, as patron of the kings of Bubastis grew in popularity and is thought to have reached a peak of popularity about the 4th Century BC It is easy to imagine the scene as her devotees came to the annual festival by the hundred thousand. Most travelled by decorated barges, with much singing and dancing to the accompaniment of the Sistrum and flutes. The people on the river banks joined in the festivities, singing and dancing and running behind the barges of the pilgrims. On the day of the annual festival the town was decorated and the grand procession of pilgrims wound through the streets. It is recorded by Heroditus that they consumed more wine at the festival than was drunk during the rest of the year. Large numbers of statuettes of the goddess were consecrated at the splendid temple. When a venerated cat died its body was mummified and ceremoniously buried. To kill a cat, even accidentally, was punishable by death. The Sistrum was played rather like a tambourine today. It was shaped like an Ankh, but minus the horizontal line. In the arched head of the instrument were three or four horizontal bars on which were arranged several sets of small cymbals, and it was these that provided the sound when the Sistrum was played. Often a small effigy of a cat was incorporated at the top of the handle.

Cat worship and respect spread across what is now Europe, from Egypt, both as a religion and as a tribal totem. The tribal totem was carried at the front of a marching column when the tribes moved from one area to another. It was in the form of a cat head, mounted on a high pole, and held by what would be a Standard Bearer. As the tribe progressed through foreign lands, often doing battle with their inhabitants, the Tribal Totem, of necessity, would be modified to take on a more aggressive appearance. In the case of a Cat Totem, the obvious modification would be to enlarge the mouth and exaggerate the length and number of teeth.

It has been suggested by Dr. L.A. Waddell in *The Pheonician Origin of the Britons, Scots & Anglo-Saxons* that these people were of Aryan-Hittite or *Khatti* stock. He deciphered an inscription on the Newton Stone in the North of Scotland in parallel Celtic-Ogham-Phoenician lettering.

These Khatti, carrying their cat totems before them, landed from boats in the South West of Britain, having crossed Gaul. Many landed in Cornwall and the coast of Dorset and then gradually worked their way northwards.

One important group worked their way northwards from Cornwall inland while others preferred a sea route. The latter would have sailed up the River Dee and thus had direct access to Chester. These people would have carried the "Cheshire Cat" totems in front of them when they entered the area. As they moved ever northwards to their northernmost refuge, the territory was named after the tribe: 'Catness' was this final settlement. It simply meant 'Headland of Cats' and to this day is known as Caithness, or more formally, as Caithness & Sutherland. The Gaelic name of Shetlands & Caithness is 'Cat'; and the Keiths or Cats have also left their name in Inchkeith and Dalkeith and to this day every Caithness or Sutherland man is 'Catach'. The Gaelic title of the Duke of Sutherland is Diuc Chat; which translated means: 'The Duke of the Cats.'

On their way north through England the Cat Tribe, as we will now call them, settled in the following places, which to this day retain their name:

Catford – The cats ford; Catworth – lived in by Cat people, a village. Chatsworth, Derby – Ceattas village. (1276) Catshill, Staffs. – The Cat people's burial mound, and many hundreds more. Gordon Cartlidge states that the population of England in AD 600 was one million and of these a vast number were called Ceatta (Cat). He believes that this was the tribal designation, and not a name as we know it.

The Khatti people would of course have been familiar with the Egyptian Cat Goddess; and this religious factor would have been incorporated with their Tribal Cat Totem.

A similar conjunction of animal totem and religious entity can be drawn between the Norse Goddess Frigg or Freya, who is celebrated every week by her day Friday (Frigg's Day). She was the Norse Goddess of the Dawn and Fertility. She is sometimes depicted being drawn through the sky in her chariot by two rather charming looking cats. (Fig. 15).

Nebo, the ancient Assyrian-Babylonian God of learning, who was the son of Marduk and very indirectly through association via Toth, Hermes, Mercury to Freya, had a Pig as his sacred animal. The above shows how a God can relate to Babylonian, Egyptian, Greek, Roman to Norse mythology! The Roman God Hermes can be dated to approximately 500 B.C. There is a further link between the pig as a sacred animal, in that as well as being sacred to Nebo it was used as a steed by Fro-Freya. (Fig. 16) Fro-Freya was the Norse God of Sun and Growth. There is a Biblical reference to Nebo: Isaiah Ch. 46, verse 1: "Bel boweth down, Nebo stoopeth, their idols were upon the beasts."

Thus we have the Cheshire Cat Tribe, descended from the ancient Khatti peoples, living happily in Cheshire and finally, in Caithness; complete with their ancient religious and totem tribe emblems of the Grinning Cheshire Cat. The religious rites, for the most part, have been depressed by the Christian Church, but the Cheshire Cat remains. In the words of a very ancient inscription on a grave in Thebes: "The beautiful cat endures and endures."

HE WAS bORN AT + +
DARESbURY PARSONAGE,
JAN, 27, 1832, AND DIED
AT GUILDFORD, JAN. 14, 1898.

13p
Alice's Adventures in Wonderland
The Year of the Child

Above: Fig. 1:
Cheshire Cat church window
at Daresbury.

Left: Fig. 2:
The Tenniel Cheshire Cat.

Above: Fig. 3:
The Arthur Rackham
Cheshire Cat.

Left: Fig. 4:
Ye Cheshire Cat after Tenniel.

YE CHESHIRE CAT.

Hugh E.
Azure, a wolf's head erased Argent.

Richard.
Gules, crusily Or, a wolf's head erased Argent.

Right: Fig. 5:
Arms of the Norman
Earls of Chester.

Randle E.
Or, a lion rampant Gules.

Randle EE.
Gules, a lion rampant Argent.

Hugh EE.
Azure, six garbs Or, 3, 2, and 1.

Above: Fig. 6: The "Red Cat" of Brimstage.

Below: Fig. 7: The sandstone Brimstage cat.

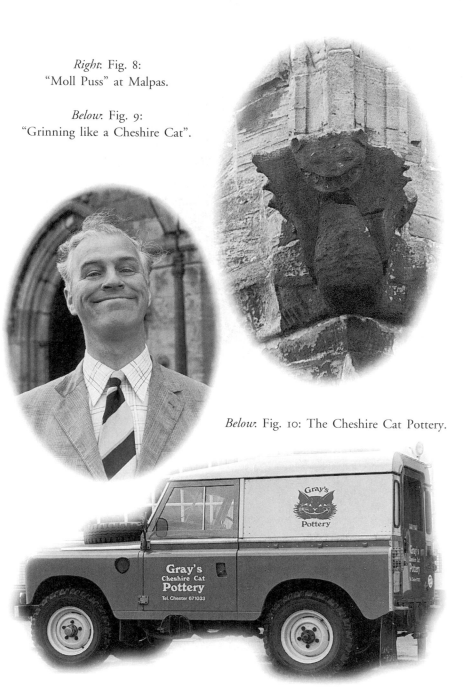

Right: Fig. 8:
"Moll Puss" at Malpas.

Below: Fig. 9:
"Grinning like a Cheshire Cat".

Below: Fig. 10: The Cheshire Cat Pottery.

Above: Fig. 11: Large Gray's Cheshire Cat.

Below: Fig. 12: Assorted pottery Cheshire Cats.

Above: Fig. 13: The Grappenhall Cheshire Cat.

Right: Fig. 14:
The Oxaca Cheshire Cat.

Right: Fig. 16:
Fro-Freya, riding her sacred pig.

Below: Fig. 15:
Frigg being drawn by her cats.

Fig. 17: Felis
Catus Cheshire.

Above: Fig. 18: Ffinlo, the Sacred Cat of Burma.

Below: Fig. 19: Pangur Ban. Sacred Cat of Burma.

Fig. 20: Pangur Ban on Cass Spane Rock I.O.M.

Chapter Four

The Vanishing Cheshire Cat

ONE OF THE WELL KNOWN CHARACTERISTICS of a Cheshire Cat is its ability to vanish; sometimes rapidly and completely, and sometimes slowly or partially. This characteristic is well illustrated by the documented famous; "Winge Cat", so named after its owner Mrs Winge.

At Congleton in Cheshire, which is about 20 miles as the crow flies from Daresbury in Cheshire, the ghost of a white cat has been observed by numerous people, sitting on a post, near the remains of Congleton Abbey. Initially recorded in literature at the beginning of this century, the cat was observed at the end of the 19th century and into the 20th. Initial sightings were recorded before the time of Lewis Carroll, and it may have been a prototype for his story of *Alice in Wonderland*.

The cat was the pet of Mrs Winge, who was the housekeeper at the old Congleton Abbey. The story goes that the cat returned home to its mistress one evening in spectral form. It sat on the steps of her cottage but refused to go inside. When Mrs Winge urged it to enter, it slowly vanished. This process was repeated every evening, no matter how many observers were present, and was witnessed by numerous friends and neighbours. Latterly, the cat took to sitting on the post near the remains of the abbey. When approached by humans, it would jump into the air and disappear!

Cats were often used as Familiars and their names are well documented, some of the most famous are: Pyewackett, Ilemauser, Holt, (1647). These names were elicited from witches by the notorious self styled Witch Finder General. A black and white familiar was called Inges and a large black cat called Gibbe. These names were obtained from their witch owners, often under extreme torture, as it was considered important to obtain the name of a familiar so that it could be called by name and so have some of its power neutralized. In 1566 the witch's familiar cat belonging to the well known witch Elizabeth Francis, who was tried at a well documented witch trial in Chelmsford, was called Sathan. Sathan, a white spotted cat, had the ability to talk. This cat could speak in a strange hollow voice which only the witch could understand. Amazingly this witch, in spite of the fact that Sathan had procured two husbands for her, to say nothing of several sheep and other feats, exchanged him with a neighbour, one Agnes Waterhouse, in exchange for a cake, together with detailed instructions for his maintenance! Sathan at this time was some 15 years old, a very good age for a cat. Like many witches' Familiars Sathan could 'Shape Change', and an example of this is contained in the record of his owner's trial. Elizabeth Francis was not happy with the husband that Sathan had procured for her, and after a row she asked Sathan to lame him for her. This he did by changing into a toad, and crawling into the husband's shoe! In spite of her confession to two murders Elizabeth Francis was only sentenced to a year's imprisonment. Elizabeth Waterhouse, Sathan's second owner, was hanged, having changed poor Sathan permanently into a toad!

Most witches' familiar cats were capable of disappearing at the appropriate time and also Shape-Changing into other creatures. The witches themselves could change into the likeness of their familiars and so carry out their nefarious deeds undetected. So it will be realized that a disappearing and rematerialising cat was a well documented and believed-in phenomenon in days of old. (This is often referred to as Shape-Shifting in various documented accounts.)

During the notorious Salem witch trials in America, in the state of Massachusetts in 1692, one witness affirmed that he was attacked by a she-devil, in the form of a witch's cat. This cat had entered by a window and seized him by the throat, lay on him for some time, and almost killed him. As soon as he called on the Trinity the cat leapt from the floor and flew out via the window.

In France magical cats were called "Matagots", and were reputed to bring nothing but good fortune to the owners of houses in which they were suitably cosseted.

In Japan the evil type magical cats were supposed to be readily identified by the fact that they were supposed to have twin tails! Some of these Japanese cats had the unfortunate habit of vampirism.

Isobel Gowdie, a witch located in Auleearn, confessed to the art of Shape-Shifting in Scotland in 1662. She confessed to turning herself into a hare and a crow, and for recreational purposes into a cat. The precise incantation used for this feat was quoted as follows:

"I shall go intil a cat
With sorrow and sych and a black shot
And I shall go in the Devil's name
Aye while I come home again."

While transformed into her cat form, the witch stated that, with her fellow coven members, she spent most of her time caterwauling and scratching and on reverting to her human form, was often covered in scratches. When in shape-changed cat form the coven visited neighbours' houses, and after making the incantation: "I conjure thee, Go with me", the inmates of the house were similarly shape-changed into cats.

In 1935 there was a report of a Vanishing Cat by J. Simpson in *The Sussex Magazine*. A Mr Crowhurst caught an animal in the dark in the garden of a house that was reputed to be haunted by a witch. He called for a light, so that he could see what he was holding. When the light was brought, it was seen that his hands were completely empty.

On a pamphlet by Dr. Lambs Darling, published in 1653, there is an account of a trial of one Anne Bodenham before Baron Wilde; a maid servant gave evidence that she had been sent to fetch "Malific Impliments" for her; before leaving the house of her employer, the witch asked the maid to come and live with her, promising that she could learn some witchcraft skills. The maid asked for an explanation, and the witch then turned herself into a large black cat, and then lay along the chimney piece. The maid was so frightened that the witch reverted to her normal form forthwith.

In the seventeenth century the practice of Shape-Shifting was fully believed in, and there are numerous references to the practice in the literature of the time.

An article appeared in the *Daily Telegraph*, together with the inevitable Tenniel drawing in July 1992, giving an account of the theory by a Mr Joel Birenbaum of Chicago, who with the International Lewis Carrol Society, had knelt at the altar of St Peter's Church, Droft, near Darlington. He saw a crudely carved cat on a wall panel, which as he moved downwards, began to disappear. When in the kneeling position, only the grin remained. The article, of very recent origin, at least shows the continuing interest in the Disappearing Cat.

Chapter Five

The Celtic Cheshire Cat Connection

THE CELTIC CONNECTION IS EXTREMELY OBSCURE, but there is some available information on three inter-related Cat Goddesses, namely Cat-Anna, Black Annis and Hog-Annaa.

Black Annis was supposed to have her bower in a cave in the Dane Hills, supposedly clawed out with her own formidable talons. This witchlike hag was reputed to lie in wait for children who strayed from home. She had long hair and yellow fangs. Black Annis would seize straying children, skin them alive and then eat them. She would scatter their bones around her cave and hang the skins on the boughs of a nearby old oak tree. It has been postulated that Annis in this semi-cat like form could have been associated with Anu, the wife of the Celtic Sky God, whose name was Ludd.

The legend of Black Annis is often related to the Celtic Cat God Cat-Anna; it is thought that Cat-Anna, might have come to Cheshire, and so to Leicestershire and the Dane Hills, via the Isle of Man, where the strange chant, sung in Manx on All Hallows Eve, was common in 1909. This chant, translated into English, and containing a reference to a Grinning Witch-Cat, contains the following:

> "Hog-Annaa – I went to the well,
> Trolla-laa – and drank my fill
> Hog-Annaa – On my way back,
> Trolla-laa – I met a Witch-Cat;
> Hog-Annaa – The Cat began to Grin ..."

The precise meaning of this chant is unknown, though it has been suggested that the second character is perhaps a Norse derived Troll.

It must be remembered that the Manx Buggane and Phynnodderees, the local mystic spirits, were well known for their powers of Shape-Shifting, and were of course particularly potent at All Hallows Eve.

On the Isle of Man, as in England and America and many other countries, it is a common practice to carry a pole, surmounted by a Grinning Cat's head, with prominent teeth, and often illuminated from inside with a candle. This is made from a large turnip in the Isle of Man, and from a pumpkin in the USA, the pole dating from the Tribal Totem times and the grinning head relating to the Cheshire Cat, with its long neck, as often depicted in latter times.

Chapter Six

Felis Catus Cheshire

IT IS A VERY INTERESTING AND CURIOUS FACT that there are a great number of people today, who firmly believe that there is in the world a real living biological Cheshire Cat. I have often been asked, by seemingly intelligent people, such questions as: "Are there many of this breed in the world?" – "Are they endangered?" – "Do you breed them?" – "What type of markings have they?" and many others! Perhaps even some of my readers have thought like this! Very sadly I have to report that there is no such creature alive today, or even in the past. It is indeed a most charming idea and shows what a hold the idea of a real live Cheshire Cat has upon the imagination of many people. If it were possible to have such a Cheshire Cat as a household pet, I would certainly be the first to have one! As it is, the best I can do is to have a collection of Cheshire Cats in sculptural form, together with several fine pictures of Felis Catus Cheshire.

In 1981 Kodak Ltd produced a remarkably fine photo of what is probably the nearest thing we are likely to see to the much desired real live Cheshire Cat, The Felis Catus Cheshire! (Fig. 17) It shows a lovely long haired Red Persian cat, in a couchant pose, exhibiting its wide Cheshire Cat mouth to perfection. It is a most amiable looking feline, and not showing its teeth in the photo. Kodak say it has just swallowed the cream; but perhaps it is one of the "Cheeser Cats" and has just consumed a large and succulent Cheshire Cheese! I am indebted to them for permission to reproduce the photo and to share the sight of this exceedingly rare creature with you.

Above: Fig. 21:
Stoneware Cheshire Cat, by Michelle Toon,
made to special commission.

Right: Fig. 22:
Bronze Cheshire Cat 7¼″ high.

Above: Fig. 23:
"The Grinning Cat".
Watercolour by F. Hughes.

Left: Fig. 24:
"The Cheshire Cat –
Always Smiling" 1907 Post Card.

Above: Fig. 26:
Manx Cheshire Cat on
Scarf. (Manx Museum).

Right: Fig. 25:
"Cheshire Cat"
Watercolour by
F. Hughes.

Left: Fig. 27:
"Ye Cheshire Cat".

Below: Fig. 28:
Left: Wooing Salt-Glazed;
Right: Christina Gray C/Cats.

EX LIBRIS

Left: Fig. 29:
Ex Libris. Pipe smoking Cheshire Cat.

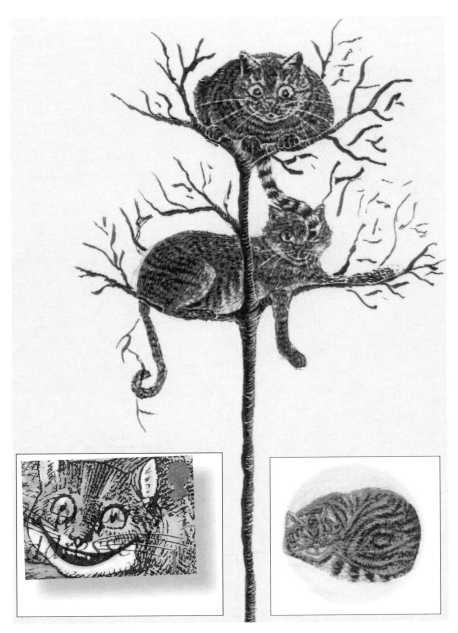

Main Picture: Fig. 30: Two Miniature Cheshire Cats in Tree.
Inset right: Fig. 31: Miniature of Cheshire Cat, curled up.
Inset left: Fig. 32: 20p Cheshire Cat head on a stamp

Left: Fig. 33:
Alice and the Cheshire Cat.

Below Left: Fig. 34:
"The Grin".

Below Right: Fig. 35:
The Duchess with the Baby.

9

Find the 'Fish·Footman'
and the 'Frog·Footman.'

5

Nº 27. THE GRIN.

Nº 15.
THE DUCHESS WITH BABY.

Below and Right: Fig. 36: Cheshire Cat Brooch (below) and painted stone Cheshire cat (right).

Above: Fig. 37: Grinning Trio of Manx Surby Cheshire Cats.

Right: Fig. 38:
Manx Cheshire Cat from
Onchan (top) and Brazen
Cheshire Cat (stood).

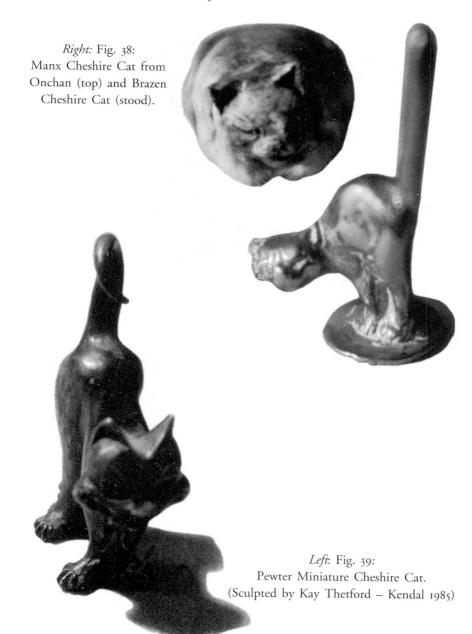

Left: Fig. 39:
Pewter Miniature Cheshire Cat.
(Sculpted by Kay Thetford – Kendal 1985)

Chapter Seven

Cheshire Cats in the Newspapers

THE CHESHIRE CAT AND ITS FAMOUS GRIN continue to this day in popular parlance and both are frequently used in newspapers and other periodicals to indicate enigmatic or unexplainable phenomenon. A particularly charming example of this occurred in the *Financial Times*, when on Monday 1st April, under 'Foreign Affairs', it printed in 1985: "A Cheshire Cat's Nuclear Strategy." This was in lettering ½″ high, on Sunday June 30th 1991, *The Sunday Express* used ¾″ letters to print a headline reading: "Cheshire Cat Smile". It will be noted that, in this instance, the usual grin has been replaced by the more mellow sounding smile. The *Daily Telegraph* in 1980, on Monday 11th August, used ¼″ letters to print: "Cheshire Cat Races Home By A Mile". All these quotations serve to illustrate that the Cheshire Cat is still very well known to most people, and is still referred to in contemporary language.

Chapter Eight

The Antiquarian and Literary Cheshire Cat

ONE OF THE FIRST LITERARY REFERENCES to the cat in profane history is by Herodotus, the father of historians, in his account of Egypt; and they are mentioned, according to Mr Blyth, in Sanskrit writings 2000 years old. Herodotus speaks of them as diminishing the vermin infesting human dwellings and also states some of the Egyptian superstitions relating to them, together with some observations upon their breeding, and dispositions. The celebrated naturalist Temminck, in his monograph of the genus Felis, adduces strong reasons for believing that the cat was originally domesticated in Egypt, and that the Gloved Cat (F. Maniculata) of Egypt and Nubia is, in all probability, the original stock of the domestic cat, though the race has been greatly modified by frequent crossing.

In Greek it is called 'ailouros', said to denote the waving of the tail. It is from this word that the present 'Ailourophile' word, meaning 'Cat Lover' is descended. In Latin it was called Catus, from the adjective signifying cunning or subtle. According to Varro, this subjective is in fact a Sabine and not a Roman word, but we find it used by Horace in his ode *Ad Mercurium*, thus its admission into the classic vocabulary can scarcely be denied. From the name Catus, is derived the English name Cat, the German Katz, and the French Chat etc.

We have seen how cats were mummified by the Egyptians in Egypt, at the time of the Goddess Bast; this tradition was revised in the year 1374, on the death of the famous Italian poet and scholar, Francesco Petrarch. (1304–1374).

Petrarch, who wrote numerous poems, inspired by his loved Laura, finally died after retirement at Arqua. In his latter years his chief companion was his much loved cat. A few days after his death Francesco de Brossano, Petrarch's son-in-law, had the cat put to death and embalmed. Today the mummified body of this historic cat lies in a niche of the room, where it was placed at the time.

On a marble slab below there is a Latin inscription, said to be by the great poet himself, stating the cat to have been: "Second only to Laura". On the other hand, Antonio Querenghi of Padua (1546–1633) a fellow poet, and friend of Tassoni, is credited with an inscription, which read:

> "Maximus ignis ego;
> Laura secundus erat."

This pleasing verse can be translated: I (Meaning Petrarch) have the greatest affection (for the cat). (Thus) Laura was Second.

Julius Caesar probably brought the domesticated cat to England in 54 BC, but at this date there were European Wild Cats inhabiting the country. These foreign cats crossed with the indigenous wild cats, and so the first domestic English cats were propagated. In spite of the numbers of wild cats in the English forests, the domestic cat was a rarity even a thousand years later.

An anonymous Irish monk wrote the charming poem: *Pangur Ban*, after whom the author named his much loved Sacred Cat of Burma (A Blue point Birman.) The original poem was of course in Irish Gaelic, but a translation of one verse is as follows:

> So in peace our tasks we ply,
> Pangur Ban, my cat, and I,
> In our arts we find our bliss,
> I have mine and he has his.

My Pangur Ban (1981–1989) has sadly gone to join his famous namesake and his place as castle cat has been taken by another sacred

Cat of Burma, with the Manx name of Ffinlo (A Seal point Birman.) who has been overseeing the writing of this book.

It was illegal to export cats from Egypt, however they gradually found their way to other countries. In the 5th century cats were recorded as popular in Persia, with a mixed descent from the Steppe cat; they were also kept in India, Burma and Siam. The cat was highly esteemed by Mohammedans, Buddhists and Hindus. We know that cats were common in China in 1000 BC and from there were subsequently introduced into Japan, often being kept in temples. Go-To-Ku-Ji in Japan is famous for its cat temple which is decorated with images of cats. Images of the cat, in various materials, are sold at the door of the temple, for presentation at the altar. This Japanese cat, Maneki-Neko, is always represented with its right paw raised to the height of its eye. It represents Happiness, Luck and Good Health. The Japanese still use the ancient name "Mau" for a cat, as originated in Egypt.

Mohammed, the prophet, had a favourite cat called Muezza. The Romans used the cat as a symbol of liberty. In Wales, cats were of considerable value, which was determined according to law.

The Sacred Cat of Burma, which is nowadays called a Birman, has a long and very interesting history which is shrouded in mystery. They, like other Sacred cats before them, were strictly guarded, and their exportation was forbidden. These cats have a head more like a Persian than a Siamese. The fur is long and silky, eyes are deep blue, the coat is slightly golden in colour. Their most distinctive feature is the white tips to the fore-paws, and white 'gauntlets' to the rear. A fine ruff completes the beautiful aspect, set off by the Blue or Seal Chocolate Points and mask.

These Sacred Cats, descended from the temple cats of Burmese legend, are the descendants of the temple cats kept as oracles in the far distant past.

In days of old, before the time of the Buddha, in the Temple of Lao-Tsun in the mountains of Lugh in Indo-China, there lived a very old priest of the Kittahs (also known as Khmers), by the name of

Mun-Ha, who had a white cat called Sinh for his oracle. Together they would sit in the temple gazing at the statue of the Goddess with the sapphire eyes, Tsun-Kyankse, who presided over the transmigration of souls. One day the old priest died suddenly, in front of the goddess, worn out by worry for his country, which was threatened by invasion. As he died, the cat, Sinh, jumped on to the sacred throne and rested against the silvery white head of his old master, and then the miracle of transmigration took place. Instead of remaining white, his fur became the golden colour of the statue, his previously yellow eyes became the sapphire blue of the goddess's, and his paws and ears turned dark brown like the ground, except for the tips of the paws which were touching the head of his dead master, they alone remained white.

When the other priests entered the chamber he compelled them, by his gaze, to go and repel the invaders who had so worried his master, and this they did. He refused all food and water, and after seven days he died, taking with him the perfect soul of his master. Another seven days followed and while the Kittahs were assembled before the goddess to decide who should be the next high priest, the hundred temple cats, who were now no longer white, but had become the same colouring as the dead Sinh, came in and surrounded Ligoa, the youngest of the priests, and so he was chosen. Since this time, whenever one of the Temple's Sacred Cats dies, the soul of a priest is supposed to go with it to Paradise.

Major Russell Gordon, serving with the British forces in the Far East (1916–1919), while protecting the last of the Kittahs, was the first to observe the Sacred Cats and also marvel at the underground temple of Lao-Tsun, built at the start of the 18th Century by the Khmer priests, whose religion was guarded and kept secret from the common people and all outsiders. The temple was situated to the east of Lake Incaougji, between Magaoug and Sembo, in an almost desert region, surrounded by barriers of insurmountable walls. There still lived in 1898 the last of the Kittahs, and he was allowed to observe a few of them with their sacred cats. After the rebellion, at the time of the English occupation of the base at Bhamo, a base quite isolated by reason of its distance from Mandalay, he was ordered to protect the Kittahs from a Brahmin invasion; this mission was a success, the Kittahs being saved from certain massacre and pillage. The Kittah Lama, Yotag-Rooh-Oughi, in gratitude gave him a plagnette depicting the Sacred Cat at the feet of a strange Deity, whose eyes were made of two elongated sapphires, and afterwards, as a mark of special favour, let him see the hundred sacred cats.

The Sacred Cats of Burma, or Birmans from the temple, found their way to France, as a pair of Sacred Cats were reputed to have been given to Major Russell Gordon between 1916 and 1919 by the Kittahs, in gratitude for his efforts in saving their temple. The cats were actually sent to France and into the care of Major Gordon and his friend, August Pavie. The male cat died during the voyage, but the female was in kitten, and thus breeding began.

An alternative source of information states that (according to Professor Jumand 1926) Mr Vanderbilt, an American millionaire, obtained the first pair of cats, while cruising in the Far East, from a dishonest servant, who had stolen the cats from the temple of Lao-Tsun. Mr Vanderbilt then gave the cats to a Mme. Thadde Hadisch in Nice in 1920. The male had died on the boat, but the female gave birth to kittens. Mother cat was called Sita, after the original temple cat in the legend, and one of her kittens named Poupee was supposedly bred to a Laotian Lynx, which belonged to a local doctor. The exact identity of the mysterious "Laotian Lynx" has never been ascertained; but it is the author's considered guess that it may have been a cross between a Siamese and a Persian type cat. I have asked Ffinlo, my Birman, but he is completely non-committal on the subject, so we may never know! In the words of an old English saying: "It's enough to make a cat laugh!"

The Sacred Cat of Burma forms yet one more strand that builds the foundations of the rope forming the background to the Cheshire Cat. It is the continued religious and magical significance of the various feline entities from the dawn of history, right up to the present time. One of the most interesting characteristics of the Sacred Cat of Burma is its ability, unlike most other breeds, to breed true from one generation to the next. They have been bred, in Europe alone, for the past fifty years. It is interesting to visualise the line of descent. Firstly, starting with Ffinlo, there are the initial five generations of Champion Birman cats, as per his pedigree, then back through successive further champions to Sita and Poupee, the first Birmans to be seen in Europe, and so on back to the temple cats of the sacred temple of Lao-Tsun in Burma. No one knows exactly where these temple cats originated, but it would be an educated guess to surmise that they might have been originally bred from the mating of a Seal-Point Siamese with a White Persian in the dim past. With the benefit of selective breeding, after many generations, the Sacred Cats of Burma would evolve. Fig. 18 depicts my cat Ffinlo, a Seal-Point Sacred Cat of Burma.

In ancient Egypt the curled up cat was the symbol of eternity, representing a circle with no beginning or end. In the Seventy-five Praises of Ra, inscribed on the royal tombs at Thebes, proclaimed Ra the creator cat god to be: 'The great cat, the avenger of the gods, the judge of words ... the governor of the holy circle', Ra represented good against evil, and every day slew the snake of darkness. Ra, the sun god, in due course, was given a wife in Egyptian mythology, with the appropriate name of Rat.

In later times cat worshippers were persecuted by the Christian Church up to the fifteenth century, when Pope Innocent VIII ordered an Inquisition to search out cat worshippers and have them burnt as witches.

Fortunately, numerous well known and famous persons throughout history have been champions of the cat. A few random examples are given as follows:

Mark Twain wrote: "A house without a cat, and a well fed, well petted and properly revered cat, may be a perfect house, perhaps, but how can it prove its title?"

The Home Office have a Manx Cat, called Peta, who was presented to them by the Lieutenant Governor of the Isle of Man in 1964. He followed a succession of Home Office cats, mostly male and all named Peter since the year 1883. Official cats are also employed by the London Museum and the Wallace Collection.

In the *Daily Mail* (28/11/1990) appeared a photo of Humphrey, the Downing Street cat. He continued in office irrespective of the change to John Major, as Prime Minister. Humphrey was on the Cabinet Office Staff List.

Ffinlo was elected to the board of Fisher Enterprises Ltd., in 1990, to act as the Vice Chairman of the company, by an unanimous vote on 29/11/1990, and has served ever since attending all company meetings, and giving flawless advice at all times!

Monsignore Capecelatro (1744–1836), the ex Bishop of Taranto, had numerous cats in his household, and at meal times they sat at table and were attended by his butler. A famous drawing by Landseer, published in Italy in 1839 depicted the scene. Queen Victoria's doctor wrote of the Archbishop and his cat, that it was magnificent and the chief member of the household. He remembered the cat and Archbishop sitting together and felt the cat was the more austere theologian of the two!

The poet, William Cowper, (1731–1800) was one of hundreds of poets to write about the cat:

> A Poet's cat, sedate and grave,
> As poets well could wish to have,
> Was much addicted to inquire,
> For nooks to which she might retire.

The above is just the commencing lines of a charming lengthy poem, which it is very easy for all cat lovers to identify with.

The grey cat, Slippers, was a special favourite of President Roosevelt of America. He was the White House Cat, and was a six toed or Polydactyl cat, often referred to as a magical lucky witch's cat.

Hillaire Belloc, in his *Bad Child's Book of Beasts* wrote (1870–1953):

But son control your actions that
Your friends may all repeat,
'This child is dainty as the cat,
And as the owl discreet.'

Kate Greenaway (1846–1901) wrote the following interesting riddle:

Three tabbies took their cats to tea,
As well behaved tabbies as well could be:
Each sat in the chair that each preferred,
They mewed for their milk, and they sipped and purred.
Now tell me this (as these cats you've seen them)–
How many lives had these cats between them?

In the 19th century 180,000 cat mummies from the cat cemetery at Beni Hassan were shipped to Liverpool. The year was 1890, and they were sold either as curios or fertiliser. The heads sold for 4/6*d*. (22½p) and the bodies for 5/6*d*. (27½p). Only one of these mummies was obtained by the British Museum. The cats in ancient Egypt were mummified and placed in cases made from woven straw, wood or bronze. Sometimes the cats' heads on the mummy cases had eyes inlaid with gold, silver, lapis lazuli and obsidian. The last is natural volcanic glass, and balls fashioned from this material are said to possess magical powers and to be one of the materials used by dragons to make their magic play ball, as depicted on all Chinese Dogs of Foo. (Males only.)

An important connection with the Christian Church was the Abbess of Nevilles in Brabant. (Died AD 659) She was a great cat lover; and subsequently became the Patron Saint of Cats. (She had a secondary role, as the saint of Gardeners). It is thus that St. Gertrude's Day is celebrated every year by cat lovers on her special day, which is the 17th of March.

Perhaps a Manx saying is appropriate at this juncture:

"Little by little, the cat ate the herring".

It means: Patience is a virtue, and infers that some time is required to piece together all the component strands of information that have gone into the make-up of the Cheshire Cat, not the least of which is a large measure of feline humour! To understand the complete Cheshire Cat it is only necessary to illustrate the way it is seen through the eyes of various artists and sculptors, and the final part of this little monograph is given over to this purpose, with photographs of the various Cheshire Cat portrayals which I have been able to collect over the years. All fill the essential definition given earlier in this book, but have the advantage that they can be seen in either two or three dimensional form!

Chapter Nine

Cheshire Cats in Art & Sculpture

Apart from the Grappenhall Cheshire Cat (Fig. 13) mentioned previously, early Cheshire Cat depictions are relatively rare, but most of the important works have been covered in the foregoing. However, about the turn of the present century, Cheshire Cat art and sculpture became much more popular, and began to proliferate. An assorted selection, from the author's extensive collection, follows:

Fig. 21 shows a very fine and original stoneware Cheshire Cat, by the Hertfordshire sculptress Michelle Toon. It is larger than most, and is 13¾″ high. It was made to special order and is black flaked on a brown ground colour. It was produced in 1980.

Fig. 22 is a photo of a very unusual Bronze Cheshire Cat, standing some 7¼″ high. This cat was reputed to have belonged to the Queen's Jeweller, being purchased when the contents of his house were sold. It has no maker's or foundry marks but is in the Art Nouveau Style and is probably circa 1920.

Fig. 23 is a watercolour entitled *The Grinning Cat* and was painted by the cat artist, F. Hughes. This charming work, dated 1982, shows no less than seven Cheshire Cats in a sailing boat, *The Grinning Cat*. The stern is inscribed: "Sailing Daily from Chester". A small Cheshire Cat pennant flies at the mast head.

Fig. 24. *The Cheshire Cat – Always Smiling* is a 1907 Postcard. It is postmarked 29th October 1907, Liverpool and was produced by H. L. & Co. The card is itself a photo of a ceramic Cheshire Cat, grinning from ear to ear and winking in a rather inebriated fashion. I have in my collection a cobalt blue ceramic Cheshire Cat, produced by the Aller Vale Art Potteries, where they were produced from 1887–1901, which is the exact duplicate of the cat on the post card. Our cat was made in Newton Abbot, Devon with Aller Vale impressed on its base. It is 6¼″ high. This firm later became Aller Vale & Watcombe Pottery Co., and was based at Torquay from 1901–1962.

Fig. 25. *Cheshire Cat.* A small watercolour miniature by the cat artist F. Hughes, who also painted Fig. 23 (See above). This artist has often exhibited at the Royal Miniature Society of Painters & Sculptors at the Mall Galleries, London. Another fine Cheshire Cat artist is Sarah Albu, the contemporary animal artist, whose excellent work, *The Guardian* shows a very fierce Cheshire Cat, sitting in a tree, it is executed in mixed media gouache and crayon. (Fig. 60)

Arthur Rackham, one of the best known Cheshire Cat illustrators (Fig. 3) did the depicted ink drawing of his cat on the back of a brown luggage label. The pen and ink drawing was heightened with white wash, the overall size: 3″ × 6″. It is interesting to note that this original was subsequently auctioned in 1985 for £2,250.

The only example known to the author of a pair of 'Wooing' Cheshire Cats is shown in Fig. 28 (left). It is 4¾″ high with white salt glazed ground and features red mouth and black pupils to the eyes. It is thought to date from approximately 1912.

Ye Cheshire Cat, shown in Fig. 27, is a very thin Cheshire Cat, in Bottle Green glazed pottery. The cat is seated upright on a circular base, and 6″ in height. The base is incised 1955 and Rd 574390. The back is incised M.Y. Gander Sculptor 1910.

Fig. 26, shows a Victorian tourist's scarf, made in Douglas, I.O.M. and Fig. 29 is a 1980 Ex Libris Book Plate of a Cheshire Cat enjoying a pipe.

Miniatures

LIKE MOST ART SUBJECTS, Cheshire Cats have had miniatures made of them, both as art and sculpture.

Fig. 30 shows two miniature Cheshire Cats happily ensconced in the topmost branches of an upside-down tree. The work is finely executed in ink. Another by the same artist, F. Hughes, shows an ink drawing of a contentedly curled up Cheshire Cat. It has fine detail and is only 2.7 cm. in diameter. (Fig. 31).

In 1990 a Cheshire Cat head was used on an English 20p. stamp. (Fig. 32) Carreras, the tobacco company, at one time issued a series of 48 cards, which included three featuring the Cheshire Cat. The cats in question were approximately 1cm. long. Fig. 33 is No. 42 of this series, and is entitled: *Alice & The Cheshire Cat.* Fig. 34 is *The Grin* and Fig. 35 *Duchess with Baby*, with the Cheshire Cat in attendance. (This is No. 15 in the series. The reverse of the cards has the Arcadia Works, London. N.W.1 printed on them. Arcadia is the original of the Arcadia Mixture pipe tobacco, made famous in *My Lady Nicotine* by J.M. Barrie.)

A brown stoneware brooch, featuring the head of a Cheshire Cat, and made in Chester, is 3.5cm. long. The same company manufacture Cheshire Cat mugs. (Fig. 36)

The smallest complete ceramic Cheshire Cat in my collection was made by the sadly defunct Grays Pottery in Chester. Fig. 12, extreme left, shows this tiny cat, which in spite of its long neck is only 4.5cm tall. It is finished in a light mottled cobalt blue glaze; and marked Gray, Chester on the base.

Three earthenware Cheshire Cats, made by Mrs Brunt of the Surby Pottery, Surby, Isle of Man, are each marked with the characteristic Surby Star pattern, in white slip, and inscribed Surby I.O.M. The largest is approximately 2″ high. They are all Manx tailless Cheshire Cats. Two are modelled standing and one seated. (Dated 1983) (Fig. 37)

A 3cm high Manx Cheshire Cat, modelled by Jackie Danaher is that exception to the rule, a fat Cheshire Cat. It is finished in a pale mottled blue colour. (Fig. 38)

A pewter miniature Cheshire Cat 2.4″ high of very vicious demeanour and with a rather explicit stance was made to special commission in 1985 and donated to the author. The maker's mark appears on the base of the rear feet. It was sculpted by Kay Thetford-Kendal of Tewin, Herts. (Fig. 39)

An unusual Russian Cheshire Cat, in the form of an early Egyptian padlock, with slide-action keys, is approximately 4.5cm long. The tail, which curves over its back, removes to open the lock, which is entirely of brass construction. (Fig. 40)

Brazen Cheshire Cats

IN VICTORIAN TIMES, Brazen Cheshire Cats came into fashion and were cast as decorative and utilitarian items. Many of these Brazen cats featured bow-ties and these smartly attired cats include: (Fig. 41) toasting forks, table crumb-trays and nut crackers. The latter (Fig. 42) is modelled with its tongue protruding, with the effort of cracking nuts. It is a Stumpy, the Manx terminology for a Manx cat, with only the vestige of a stump tail, as opposed to the completely rounded back profile of the true Manx Cat.

Flat-Backed Brazen Cheshire Cats, sometimes used as fire-back cats (Fig. 43), follow the more usual long necked configuration. Some of these double as poker holders and as backing ornaments for calendars. (Fig. 44) A brazen door-knocker Cheshire Cat has a knowingly winking eye. Its front paws hold a bow to form the knocker. (Fig. 61)

A very charming Venetian bronze Cheshire Cat, painted green with yellow eyes and a pink mouth, dates to Victorian times and doubles as a paperweight cum paper clip or letter holder. It is 2¼″ long and has a strong Tenniel influence. (Fig. 45)

Small China Cheshire Cats

TENNIEL WAS THE INSPIRATION for the superbly executed small china Cheshire Cat made by the Beswick pottery by Royal Doulton. Known as the Alice Series Cheshire Cat, they were individually hand painted and numbered. The author's is No. 77 Ser. No. U2480. It is painted in

Top left: Fig. 40:
Russian lock Cheshire Cat.

Above: Fig. 41:
Cheshire Cat Brazen Toasting Fork
and Crumb Tray.

Left: Fig. 42:
Cheshire Cat Nut-Cracker.

Below: Fig. 43:
Cheshire Cat Flat Fire-Back Type (left),
Brass Manx Cheshire Cat (below).

Below: Fig. 44:
Cheshire Cat Poker
and Calendar Holders.

Left: Fig. 45:
Cheshire Cat
Venetian Letter Holder.

Below: Fig. 46:
Beswick Cheshire Cat.

Bottom: Fig. 47:
Crested Cheshire Cats;
Left: Chester;
Right: Port Erin (I.O.M.).

Left: Fig. 49:
Galle Type Cheshire Cat.

Right: Fig. 48:
White Welsen Cheshire Cat.

Left: Fig. 50:
Gloss Black Cheshire Cat, with Brown eyes.

Right: Fig. 51:
Matt Black Cheshire Cat,
with Green eyes.

Left: Fig. 52:
Manx 'Staffordshire Type'
Cheshire Cat.

Below: Fig. 53:
Blue 'Oriental Type' Cheshire Cat.

Below. Fig. 54: Bronze 'Oriental Type' Cheshire Cat

Below: Fig. 55: *Right*: Spill Holder; *Left*: Container Cat.

Fig. 56: *Above*: Shelley "Good Luck";
Right: Candle Stick.

Above: Fig. 57: Money Box Cheshire Cat
Left: Brown Pottery Cheshire Cat (1985)

Right: Fig. 58:
Cheshire Cat & Mouse

Fig. 59: "Cheeser" Cheshire Cat Postcard. 1922.

multi-tone brown on a green base. Manufactured in 1974 and purchased new in 1980. Length 3¾″ × 1¾″ high. (Fig. 46)

The Long Necked inebriated winking Cheshire Cat was often produced as giftware in crested china, the crests representing the various towns where the Cheshire Cat gifts were purchased, often by holidaymakers for gifts for those back home. I have examples (Fig. 47) bearing the crests of Port Erin in the Isle of Man and also for the City of Chester. The latter is 3½″ high and below the Chester City Coat of Arms is printed "The Cheshire Cat Always Smiling". It was made in England by Victoria China, and the base is marked: J. P. & Co. The Port Erin Crested Cheshire Cat, of similar design to the Chester one is 3¼″ high and dates from 1929–1939. It is almost the same design as the cat shown in the 1907 postcard in Fig. 24. It is probably of English Florean china.

A 3¼″ high White Cheshire Cat, with facial features delineated in black, was made by the Welsen Giftware Company in England. It (Fig. 48) bears a strong resemblance to the small brazen flat backed Cheshire Cat described above. There was a great deal of copying, particularly in Victorian times, in the configurations of Cheshire Cats. Basically they were the Long Necked, Smug Upright and Couchant Tenniel. The only item of apparel normally worn was the bow-tie and this was confined to the Long Necked and Smug Upright breeds, and then usually confined to the Brazen examples.

The captions applied to Cheshire Cats are also very traditional, being copied from one artist to another. The most common is 'The Cheshire Cat – Always Smiling'. Less common, 'As happy as a Cheshire Cat Eating Gravel' and 'He grins like a Cheshire Cat Chewing gravel'. This latter inscription is found on the 3⅜″ high Goss Cat, featuring the Dartmouth crest. Other Crested cats' mottoes read: Settle – 'The Smile that won't come off', Dover – 'Cheshire Cat – Still Smiling', London – 'Luck'.

The Greater Cheshire Cats

ONE OF THE LARGEST AND MOST IMPORTANT Cheshire Cats is the very fine cat made contemporaneously and very similar to a Faience Gallé cat. This pottery cat is decorated in Hearts and Flowers design. It is 13″ high and marked J.R. on the base. The ground colour is yellow, with blue and white embellishments, the green glass eyes are red-veined, the muzzle is white and the tail banded. A curious mark on the back of the head is perhaps a monogram incorporating a stylised "A". It is thought to date to about 1920, but could be earlier. (Gallé of Nancy manufactured cats towards the end of the 19th Century.) This fine cat was featured in *Country Life* magazine on February 14th, 1985. (No further information was forthcoming however.) Fig. 49

Large black long necked Cheshire Cats, some with painted and some with glass eyes were manufactured in Staffordshire prior to 1900. A pair of the painted eye variety, with yellow painted eyes are 9″ high. They were centrifugally moulded, and consequently have a thin wall thickness. (See Fig. 12) The Large Gray's Cat sits in the centre.

Nearly all Greater Cheshire Cats are of the long-necked configuration. An 11″ high glossy black cat, with fine brown glass eyes and traditional long neck and of superior craftsmanship to the aforementioned pair in Fig. 12, has its base marked, Made in England. When new, it was sold for the considerable sum of 24/- (£1.20)! (Fig. 50)

A fine Cheshire Cat, some 10⅜″ high, with matt black glaze, and similar to the one just described has green glass eyes, with black pupils. No. 27 is inscribed on the base and '250 Made in England' is impressed around the lower part of the moulding, just in front of the tail. The exact date is unknown, but thought to be about 1910. It was purchased from the Shillington Antiques Fair in Bedfordshire in 1980. (Fig. 51)

The unusual Manx Cheshire Cat is one of only a pair of Manx cats specially commissioned by the author and made by Rushton Pottery,

St. Johns, Isle of Man in 1984. They were made in the original 1840–1860 moulds, and decorated in the traditional Staffordshire style, with copper lustre and cream glaze. Height is 7¾″ and they are marked and dated on the base by the makers. (Note the bow around the neck.) (Fig. 52)

Chinese & Oriental Cheshire Cats

CHINESE AND ORIENTAL CHESHIRE CATS are usually modelled in the Couchant style and an excellent example is shown 3½″ high and 4¾″ long, cast in Alvastone from porcelain, originals in a private collection. The originals being of 18–19th-century origin, this cat was made by Alva Museum Replicas Inc. in New York, USA (Fig. 53)

The cast bronze cat is also a replica, but almost an exact replica of the original and cast in the same way. It is somewhat similar to the blue cat mentioned above, but with a more restrained grin. It is mounted on a contemporary carved wooden base. This couchant cat is 6″ long x 2¾″ high and was purchased from Liberty's in London. (Fig. 54)

The Working or Utilitarian Cheshire Cat

A NUMBER OF CHESHIRE CATS take time to act as workers in various forms. A black seated long necked cat 5¾″ high has its back to a pipe spill or match basket, which is incorporated in a wicker-work pattern and brownish glaze. Inside the basket and base of cat are olive drab. This cat has a long and unusually thin neck and large pointed ears. The flank is marked: *Ye Cheshire Cat.* Its toes are prominent. Approximate date is 1905. (Fig. 55 (Right))

Another 'Container Type' cat is Black, 6″ high and is seated beside a Gold/Brown container embellished with a red rim. This in turn, has a fine black coach-line below it. (Fig. 55 (Left))

The Edwardian Black Candlestick cat, with red eyes, has its tail folded back against its back, to act as a carrying handle. It has a high gloss black glaze and is 6¼″ high. (Fig. 56)

The 3¼" high black china cat, with 'Good Luck' on the side, has 'Tim' on the obverse. Its eyes are green. From the maker's mark on the base it is thought to be by Shelly of Foley and made in 1925. These cats were sometimes used as dance prizes. (Fig. 56)

A glossy black Cheshire Cat, with white eyes, in a couchant posture has a slot in its back, and is designed to act as a money box. It was made in England by Sylva & Co., and purchased in Peel, I.O.M. in 1983. It has an overall length of 6" (Fig. 57)

The exceedingly amiable earthenware cat, gently cradling a mouse in its paw; is thought to be a unique example of a Cheshire Cat & mouse. In the normal way Cheshire Cats are too busy grinning to go hunting, so it is assumed that this specimen is treating the mouse as a pet! It is in brown and green glaze 5¾" high with a maximum base at 5⅝". Made in Rabley Heath, Hertfordshire in 1981. Tabby markings. (Fig. 58)

The "Cheeser" Cheshire Cat.

CHESHIRE CATS ARE KNOWN TO BE VERY FOND OF CHESHIRE CHEESE and small cheeses from Cheshire used to be named after them. Cheshire Cheese was also moulded into the shape of Cheshire Cats, using wooden moulds.

The Cheshire Cat depicted in a postcard, posted in Chester on 15/3/1922, is sitting on a cheese, which has been labelled to avoid any misunderstanding, and photographed posing with a silk ribbon tied in a bow around her neck. The cat is in turn labelled; with the inscription *Grinning like a Cheshire Cat* to avoid any doubt about her species! This is in turn repeated as the caption for the postcard! The cat itself is fitted with well fitting glass eyes. The card was printed by the well known Valentine's company. (Fig. 59)

Fig. 60: The Guardian

Fig. 61: *Right:* Cast Bronze
Doorknocker at Woodland Towers,
Isle of Man.

Fig. 62: *Below:* The Aller Vale
Cheshire Cat 1887–1901

Chapter Ten

The Component Integrated Cheshire Cat

To SUMMARIZE, the composite Cheshire Cat is made up from the following integrated components and its salient physical features are:

The Head – this is large, and similar in conformation to that of a Persian type cat.

The Ears – these are well formed, pricked and alert.

Teeth – a multiplicity of prominent and sharp teeth.

Mouth – wide and stretching from ear to ear. Developed from the ferocious form required to frighten enemies in time of battle, and to be intimidating when used as a Tribal Totem in the past.

Neck – the neck is usually long, and was derived from the long poles used to mount the grinning ferocious head when carried at the front of a marching column of 'cat people', when the tribe, preceded by its tribal totem, moved from place to place, or marched into battle.

The Psychological attributes are as follows:

The Religious heritage – derived from the Egyptian cat goddess Bast, the Burmese goddess Tsun-Kyankse, the Celtic goddess Cat-Anna and an amalgam of other deities including input from the Norse goddess Frigg and others.

The Magical heritage – the amiable side of its nature draws heavily on the characteristics of the French Matagots. The more sinister, from

Witches' Familiars. The power to dematerialize and rematerialize at will can be attributed to the Winge Cat, and a heritage of psychical and assorted magical cats.

The above are only the principal components of this complex and exceedingly charming creature; as we have seen there are myriads of other lesser influences which, over the generations, have built up the everlasting Cheshire Cat. In artistic renderings its character is infinitely variable, depending on the skill and imagination of the artist, who sometimes accentuates its more amiable side, sometimes the enigmatic and on occasion the sinister.

To paraphrase the words of Dr Johnson, speaking of his cat Hodge, one could certainly say:

Cheshire Cats are very fine cats, very fine cats indeed!

Bibliography

Aberconway, Christabel Lady: *A Dictionary of Cat Lovers*, Michael Joseph, 1948.

Sillar & Meyler: *Cats Ancient & Modern*, White Lion, 1966.

Gettings, Fred: *The Secret Lore of the Cat*, Grafton Books, 1989.

Ralphs, E.E.: *To Make a Cat Laugh*, Shearwater Press, 1977.

Leach, Maria: *The Lion Sneezed*, Sheldon Press, 1977.

Lillington, Kenneth: *Nine Lives*, Andre Deutsch, 1977.

Anderson, Janice: *The Cat-A-Logue*, Guiness Superlatives, 1989.

Metcalf, Christine: *Cats*, Hamlyn, 1969.

Leman, J. & M.: *The Perfect Cat*: Pelham Books, 1983.

Angel, Marie: *Cherub Cat*, Angel Tiger, Pelham Books, 1988.

McClinton, K.M.: *Antique Cats for Collectors*, Lutterworth, 1974.

Briggs, K.M.: *Nine Lives, Cats in Folklore*, Routledge & Kegan Paul, 1980.

Graves, Robert: *Larousse Encyclopedia of Mythology*, Paul Hamlyn, 1959.

Carr, Samuel: *The Poetry of Cats*, Chancellor Press, 1980.

Saures, J.C.: *The Indispensable Cat*, Stewart Tabori & Chang, 1983.

Loxton, Howard: *Cats of the World*, Treasure Press, 1985,

Rawson, Jessica: *Animals in Art*, British Museum Publications, 1977.

Gardner, Martin: *The Annotated Alice*, 1970.

Saures, J.C.: *Great Cats*, Bantam Books, 1981.

Saures & Chwast: *The Illustrated Cat*, Harmony Books, 1976.

Herbert, Agnes: *The Isle of Man*, John Lane, The Bodley Head, 1909.

Foster D. & Daniel A.: *In Praise of Cats*, Musson, Toronto, 1974.

Readers Digest: *Folklore, Myths & Legends of Britain*, 1973.

Carpenter H. & Pritchard M.: *Oxford Companion to Children's Literature*, 1984.

Pear's Pets, 1913.

The Popular Encyclopedia, London, 1887.

Ralphs, E.E.: *To Make a Cat Laugh*, Shearwater Press, I.O.M., 1977.

Pond, Grace: *The Observer's Book of Cats*, Frederick Warne, 1959.

Smith, Vivienne: *The Birman Cat*, Bernard Kaymar, 1981.

Codex Sancti Pauli.